My Loc Journey

Lookbook: Volume 1

Ms. Kym

Kinky Biz ~ Ms. Kym

My Loc Journey

Lookbook: Volume 1

ISBN 978-1-7330579-9-8 (hardcover)
ISBN 979-8-218-39942-9 (soft cover)

Sivad Publishing
www.tamathaadavis.com

Photography by Forever Young Visuals
Shaylen Young
Aaron Wheatley

Printed in USA by Ingram Spark
First printing, June 2024

Kinky Biz ~ Ms. Kym

II

My Loc Journey

Lookbook: Volume 1

Ms. Kym

Table of Contents

About Kinky Biz

Kinky Biz is an all-natural loctician business owned by Ms. Kym, a master loctician with over 30 years of experience. Her exceptional skills and expertise have earned her a reputation for helping clients achieve healthy, beautiful locs that flourish under her care.

At Kinky Biz, Ms. Kym not only provides top-notch loc services, but also offers a line of all-natural specially formulated products. They are designed to promote hair growth and maintain optimal health. These products are crafted with the utmost care using high-quality ingredients that nourish the scalp and strands resulting in vibrant luscious locs.

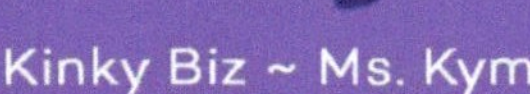

Kinky Biz ~ Ms. Kym

About Kym

Inspired by my sister-friend Stacie, thirty years ago I decided to go all-natural. She was pregnant at the time and didn't want to use a relaxer anymore due to the harmful effects it could have on her unborn child. This began my all-natural hair journey. I wore my hair in an afro for a year before another sister friend, Janine, helped me to begin my loc journey.

I loc'd my daughter's hair when she was four years old, which gave me a passion for natural hair care. This experience gave me the drive to become a master loctician. Along with my passion for doing locs, I decided to create products for hair growth. These products are for men and women to aid in healthy hair. In addition, I stay updated with hair shows and natural hair education.

Kinky Biz ~ Ms. Kym

Clients' Journeys

Aaron's Journey

One of the reasons I got locs was because of the different styles. The rope style (two-strand twists) is my favorite. I wear this style because it compliments my appearance.

I chose green because it is my favorite color. I added red to reflect my passion, energy, and enthusiasm. Having locs has taught me to have patience. Good character is not formed instantly. It's formed little by little, day by day.

I was hopping from stylist to stylist for a while. I finally met Kym, who is a master loctician. Kym made me understand how to love and take care of my locs. As she would say, "You should never get them too tight."

Kinky Biz ~ Ms. Kym

Rachel's Journey

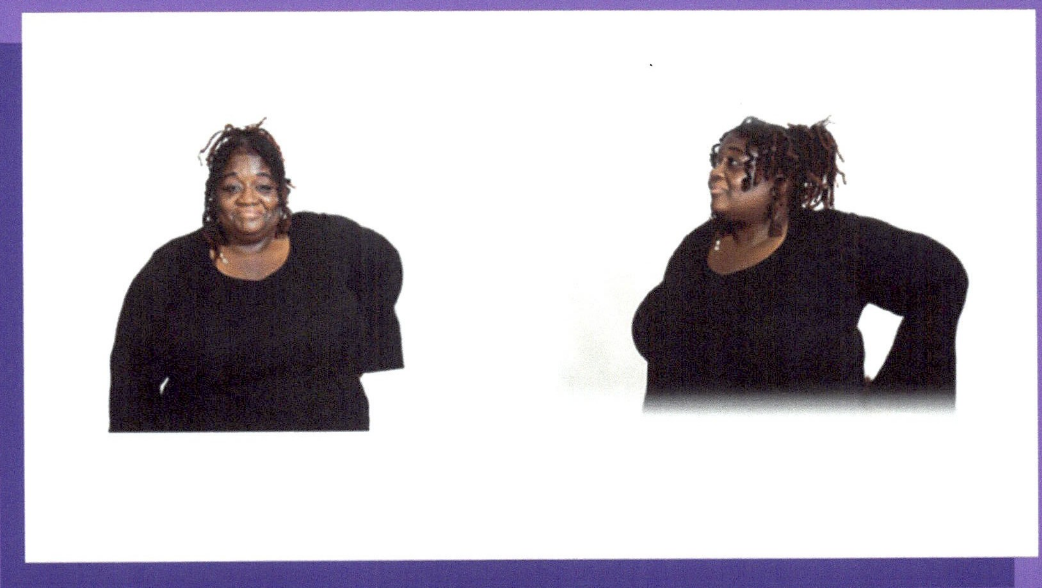

I got my locs because I was tired of believing beauty meant I had to put a relaxer in my hair for it to be beautiful. I realized my hair is beautiful in its natural state. My favorite part of the journey is the direct connection to my African roots, the hair versatility, and meeting others on this path, which has allowed me to share our loc journey stories.

I've faced adversities like society's negative biases about locs including negative remarks and assumptions about my character based solely on my hairstyle. I'm grateful that Kinky Biz and Ms. Kym have guided and empowered me on this journey.

Kinky Biz ~ Ms. Kym

Agiano, Agianee, & Isaac's Journey

Kinky Biz ~ Ms. Kym

6

My Loc Journey

Agiano

I got locs because I was tired of the natural hair journey. While I loved my hair, the maintenance and upkeep were a bit much. With a busy schedule, it was not fun that each weekend it took an entire day to do my hair with the washing, conditioning, detangling, etc.

I was referred to Kym by one of her clients. Her knowledge of locs and desire for healthy hair made me want to get locs. It was one of the best decisions in my life.

All of the loc journey phases are my favorite. In each phase, I've learned more about myself and learned to embrace myself more and be comfortable in my skin at every stage. No matter whether my hair is neat, frizzy, short, or long, my hair is beautiful. My crown is beautiful.

Agianee

I started my loc journey because I wanted a new appearance that could express who I was inside and out. My favorite part of my loc journey was every loc stage I encountered because I was able to see my hair transform.

Issac

I wanted to try something new. I have only had my locs for a short amount of time, but my peers have fully embraced them.

Ajai's Journey

I wanted locs years before I got them, but the need to conform to the corporate world kept me from getting them. The day I decided to become my own boss and never ask for another job was the day my loc journey began.

Kinky Biz ~ Ms. Kym

8

Lewis' Journey

For most of my life, I've had a bald fade. When I was younger, I wanted to grow locs but didn't understand how to "start" the process. During the pandemic, I had a lot of downtime, so this is when I finally decided to take the leap of faith and begin my starter locs. The journey to locs represents a spiritual awakening and desire to vibrate higher and connect with like-minded individuals. It's also a way to have long hair while maintaining a natural, healthy look.

My favorite part of the journey was going to Kinky Biz for my wash and retwist and being surprised by a new style from Kym. I enjoy wearing my locs down and feeling the warm rays of the Texas sun on my hair.

Kinky Biz ~ Ms. Kym

My Loc Journey

Lookbook: Volume 1

Holly's Journey

Kinky Biz ~ Ms. Kym

10

My Loc Journey

I started my loc journey in August 2019. I feel very proud of my hair and wear it with pride and confidence. It serves my life. I relinquished that control of not worrying about sweat, rain, etc. As my locs grow, I grow stronger. I'm disciplined, and my locs have been a disciplined journey. Ultimately, my locs are a physical manifestation of my inner growth and discovery.

Kinky Biz ~ Ms. Kym

My Loc Journey

Lookbook: Volume 1

JC & Ryane's Journey

My Loc Journey

Ryane

I began my natural journey about five years ago, and the maintenance as my hair grew became more and more time-consuming. I wanted something that freed up my time and effort and still made me feel beautiful.

Meeting Kym has been such a light and joy in my life. My mom and I enjoy our girls' time, and it's such a great stress relief every time we are around women and enjoy each other.

If you're thinking about it, DO IT! It is the best decision I've ever made.

JC

First and foremost, I wanted to set an example for my daughter to accept our natural hair and its beauty. I have always admired locs and the movement for our natural beauty.

My favorite part is the ritual of our maintenance. My daughter and I schedule an appointment every three weeks without fail. It's the thing we do. We ride together to our appointment, and we get pampered. There's always a lot of laughter. It nourishes our souls and our locs.

As I enter a space with all the confidence and love God has given me, there is no looking back. A big thank you to Kym, owner of Kinky Biz, for loving her craft and just simply giving a damn. We love you!

Kinky Biz ~ Ms. Kym

Jessie, Mikey & Joey's Journey

Kinky Biz ~ Ms. Kym

14

My Loc Journey

Jessie

My loc journey started because of COVID. I was paranoid about going to the barber-shop, so I let my hair grow. Finishing nursing school and catching COVID was a stress-ful time in my life. After I overcame that sickness, I was locked into the stay-at-home and safety protocol to keep me and my family safe! I originally was going to get braids, but I thought locs would look better and it would be something different!

Formerly, I was in the military, so this was the first time I did not wear a fade. Initially, I did not like them that much when they were little buds, but as they started to get longer, I knew this was a journey I could stick with!

Mikey

My youngest son has never seen a pair of clippers. Mikey would cry when we combed his hair or got it braided. Finally, I convinced my wife that this would be good for Mikey. I saw the joy and passion in his eyes whenever it was time to get retwisted. I've watched him be responsible and take care of his hair, which showed the growth that I was hoping to steer him towards!

Joey

Joey wore a fade for the longest. I asked him to try locs. He started his journey six months ago, and he absolutely loves them. Seeing my boys happy with their locs and caring for their locs has been the most important part of this journey for me!

Kinky Biz ~ Ms. Kym

Ron's Journey

My Loc Journey

Lookbook: Volume 1

The hair care and customer service profession within Kinky Biz stands out the most. I've been there from the beginning and watched Kym grow over the past 11 years. I've seen how the purple caterpillar has transformed into a beautiful multi-colored purple butterfly with her business.

I am proud to have seen her learn, ask questions, and implement all her knowledge. Kym has grown into a strong, business-minded individual with fantastic hair care, design, and excellent customer service. Additionally, Kym offers hair care products and accessories.

Keep moving forward, my Black sister!!!

Kinky Biz ~ Ms. Kym

Shaylen's Journey

My Loc Journey

Lookbook: Volume 1

My loc journey is a testament to the transformative power of self-discovery and embracing one's true identity. I had always adhered to societal expectations, keeping a clean cut throughout my life. After becoming a single father at age 20, I was forced to grind harder.

It wasn't until later in life, after obtaining my bachelor's degree in business, that I wanted to be an entrepreneur. I left an eight-year career at a Fortune 500 company to pursue entrepreneurship. Taking that leap of faith also meant embarking on a personal journey of self-expression. Growing out my hair symbolized breaking free from societal expectations and embracing my authentic self.

My loc journey has transformed my physical appearance and empowered me with newfound confidence and authenticity. Kym has helped me continue this path of self-discovery and entrepreneurship. I hope to inspire others struggling with their identity or facing social pressures. My story proves that unapologetically embracing who you are can lead to incredible personal growth and liberation from external judgments.

Kinky Biz ~ Ms. Kym

Tangie, Arie, and EJ's Journey

Kinky Biz ~ Ms. Kym

My Loc Journey
Lookbook: Volume 1

Tangie

Initially, I got locs because I love having my hair braided, and trying to locate a braider was sometimes difficult and costly. I kept being drawn to locs because my son had them, and I discovered I really liked them! I love the current phase of my hair. It is growing, and I love the styling options that come along with having locs.

Prior to getting locs, I faced adversity at first because everyone told me only homosexual women have locs. Thankfully I don't allow others to define me, so I went forth with my plan to start my loc journey.

Arie

I wanted my hair loc'd because I loved my mom's hair. My locs make me feel so beautiful, strong, and powerful. Around 8-9 months into my journey, I felt like giving up because my process wasn't going as fast as I wanted. I almost wanted my straight hair again. However now that I'm further into my journey and completely loc'd, I love my hair. I get daily compliments, and my hair makes me feel so strong and beautiful.

Ikenia's Journey

Kinky Biz ~ Ms. Kym

My Loc Journey

I first started getting my hair loc'd because I wanted to find freedom. My favorite part of my loc journey was watching my hair grow past my shoulders. It was all natural and completely mine! My most considerable adversity with my locs was overcoming my fear of what society says your hair should look like. This loc journey has taught me to change my mindset, be patient, and grow spiritually.

Kinky Biz ~ Ms. Kym

Products Page

Ja Neen
Lock Refresher

Ingredients:
rose water, hint of mint, tea tree, lemon essential oil, amber scent

Autie V
Hair Moisturizer

Ingredients:
rice bran, vitamin E, almond oil, argan oil, lemon essential oil

Tee tee
Hair Moisturizer

Ingredients:
rice bran, sunflower grape seed oil, sweet almond oil, castor oil, jojoba oil, rosemary scent

Aunt E
Hair Moisturizer

Ingredients:
rice bran, sweet almond oil, avocado oil, jojoba oil, apricot kernel, almond coconut scent

Products Page

JB
Beard Growth Oil

Ingredients:
rice bran, vitamin E, sweet almond oil, jojoba oil, sandalwood essential oil

Tra Butta
Body Intense Moisturizer

Ingredients:
argon butter, almond butter, shea butter, sweel almond oil

Grow Baby Grow
Hair Serum

Ingredients:
rice bran, sunflower grape seed oil, sweet almond oil, castor oil, jojoba oil, rosemary scent

Black Soap
Face and Body Cleanser

Ingredients:
water, cocoa pods ash, plantain skin ash, palm oil 100% vegetable based imported from Ghana

My Loc Journey
Lookbook: Volume 1

Sista Friends

Kinky Biz ~ Ms. Kym

Get in Touch

kinkybiz   kinkybizofficial   kinkybiz

www.kinkybizlocs.com